C

Willie Mays

Shaun McCormack

the rosen publishing group's
rosen central

To my grandfather, Peter Roccagli, who introduced me to the fascinating game of baseball when I was five years old.

Published in 2003 by The Rosen Publishing Group, Inc.
29 East 21st Street, New York, NY 10010

First Edition

Library of Congress Cataloging-in-Publication Data

McCormack, Shaun.
Willie Mays / by Shaun McCormack.
    p. cm. — (Baseball Hall of Famers)
Includes bibliographical references.
Summary: Examines the personal life and baseball career of the man considered by many sports experts to be the greatest baseball player of all time.
ISBN 0-8239-3604-X (library binding)
1. Mays, Willie, 1931– —Juvenile literature. 2. Baseball players—United States—Biography—Juvenile literature. [1. Mays, Willie, 1931– 2. Baseball players. 3. African Americans—Biography.]
I. Title. II. Series.
GV865.M38 M35 2003
796.357'092—dc21

                                                        2001007916

Manufactured in the United States of America

Contents

Willie Mays gets under Vic Wertz's 440-foot blast in the eighth inning of the World Series opener on September 29, 1954, at the Polo Grounds in New York City. Mays caught the ball and the Giants won the game 5–2. His catch remains one of the most memorable moments in baseball history.

Introduction

It's Game 1 of the 1954 World Series at the Polo Grounds in New York City. The score is tied at two. It's the top of the eighth inning. The Cleveland Indians have runners on first and second, with no outs. Don Liddle is on the pitcher's mound for the Giants, and Vic Wertz is batting for the Indians. Willie Mays, the Giants' twenty-three-year-old, all-star center fielder, stares in toward home plate, waiting for the next pitch.

The moment is juiced with drama.

Coaches and players in the New York dugout are on the edge of their seats. Many of them fear that the game may be slipping away from them.

The mood in the Cleveland dugout is powered with positive anticipation.

In the stands, thousands of nervous fans have fallen silent.

The players, and the 50,000 fans in attendance, know the next pitch might decide the outcome of the '54 World Series. But nobody realizes they are about to witness one of the most magical moments in the history of baseball.

Liddle hurls the ball toward home plate, and Wertz takes a mighty swing. The crack of the bat sends the ball deep toward center field. Mays spots the ball flying high in the sky. He turns his back on home plate and begins to run toward the center field fence. He looks over his left shoulder and brings his sprint to full speed, hoping he can cut off the ball before it rolls to the fence. About 440 feet from home plate, Mays extends his body and reaches out with his glove. His hat flies off his head. In one motion, Willie catches the ball, turns around, fires the ball in to second base, loses his balance, and falls to the ground.

Many fans consider Willie's miracle catch to be the best in the history of baseball. It helped the Giants escape the eighth inning without giving up a run. A home run in the bottom of the tenth

WILLIE HOWARD MAYS, JR.

261

Outfield: New York Giants
Born: May 6, 1931, Westfield, Ala. Home: Fairfield, Ala.
Ht.: 5'10½" Wt.: 170 Eyes: Brown Hair: Black
Bats: Right Throws: Right

Voted the National League Rookie of the Year in 1951, Willie was only 20 years old when he came up. He broke into pro ball with Trenton in '50 and batted .353. With Minneapolis at the start of the '51 season, Willie hit .477 in 35 games and the Gia... led him up. His first Big League hit was a ...ally great fielder, Willie went into the Army

	JE BATTING RECORDS			FIELDING RECORDS			
Home Runs	RBI	Batting Average	Put-outs	Assists	Errors	Field. Avg.
20	68	.274	353	12	9	.976
12	85	.391	310	22	6	.982

**Minor League Lifetime Record

S BASEBALL PRTD. IN U.S.A.

WILLIE MAYS

Willie Mays played with enthusiasm and exuberance while excelling in all phases of the game—power hitting, fielding, throwing, and baserunning. His staggering career statistics include 3,283 hits and 660 home runs.

inning took the Giants to a 5–2 victory in Game 1 of the '54 World Series, which they went on to win, four games to none.

In addition to winning many prestigious awards, Willie played the game with grace and skill. Tons of baseball experts say that Willie Mays was the best ballplayer of all time!

Willie Mays earned eleven Gold Gloves, played in a record-tying twenty-four
All-Star Games, and participated in four World Series.

Boyhood Baseball

Willie Mays was just six months old when his dad introduced him to the game of baseball. Willie's father, William Howard Mays, took two chairs and lined them up next to each other. He placed a baseball on one of them.

His father asked, "See the ball? See it?"

Willie would cling to one chair for balance and walk toward the chair with the baseball on it. After grabbing the ball, he'd give it back to his dad. They would play this game for hours at a time. Each time, Willie's dad would move the chairs farther apart. Eventually, Willie was waddling across the entire room to get the ball.

It was the beginning of a life that would be devoted to baseball.

Willie Mays was born on May 6, 1931, in Westfield, Alabama. Both his parents were eighteen years old and fresh out of high school when Willie was born. Willie's mother, Ann, was a track star while she was in high school. His father worked for low wages at a steel mill and struggled to provide food and shelter for his family.

Willie's folks split up when he was three years old. After the divorce, his mother married again. She had ten more children, eight girls and two boys, and died in 1953 while giving birth to her eleventh child.

By the time Willie was five, his father was bouncing balls on the sidewalk for him to catch. Willie has said that his father was never too tired to play, and they would play catch for hours every day.

William Mays played baseball for a semiprofessional team in the Birmingham, Alabama, Industrial League. Mr. Mays was a quick, agile ballplayer and earned the nickname "Cat." Willie didn't realize it at the time, but from an early age, he was picking up valuable, firsthand information about the game from his father. For young Willie, it was just a lot of fun.

When he played, William Mays brought his son to Industrial League baseball games. Willie sat on the bench with the team. He heard the grown men talk about baseball. He heard them talk about the different strategies pitchers used during a variety of situations and games. Young Willie learned how a runner on first base could take a bigger lead when there was a left-handed pitcher on the mound. He heard about how hitters changed their swings in order to move runners from first to third, and how a hitter would watch a few pitches go by if it looked like the pitcher was losing control of the strike zone.

Sometimes, Willie even went onto the field before a game to have a catch with his dad. He would run around the bases, sliding into second base, third base, and then home plate.

The lessons Willie learned from being around grown-up baseball players when he was very young gave him an edge on the kids his age when he started playing Little League.

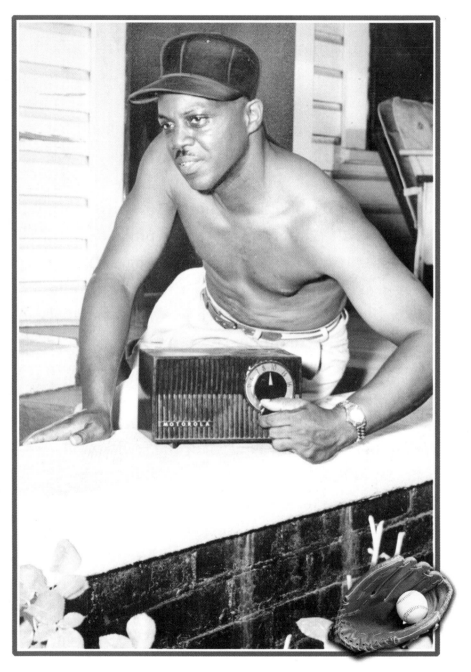

A semiprofessional ballplayer, William Howard Mays taught his son Willie valuable lessons about the game.

Bringing Willie to the games helped Willie's father, too. As Willie sat in the dugout, he was surrounded by adults. For Willie's dad, this was like having a team of baby-sitters for his son.

Willie's dad had a good friend named Otis Brooks who helped around the house when Mr. Mays was away. Willie and Otis became friends, and Willie started calling him Uncle Otis. Willie had many chores to do, and the work took time away from playing baseball and other sports. Otis had big dreams for Willie, and he ended up doing most of Willie's chores so Willie would have more time to play.

In the 1930s, two neighborhood girls named Ernestine and Sarah had been orphaned and William Mays had taken them into his home. The girls became part of the family. They did most of the cooking and cleaning, and always made sure Willie got the attention a baby needs. They made sure he was clean and well fed. In return for the things they did, Mr. Mays gave them a place to live.

When Ernestine was old enough to help support the family, she got a job waiting tables at a neighborhood restaurant. Ernestine gave Willie $10 every week so he could buy lunch when he was at school. That was a lot of money back then.

Willie had enough money to buy lunch for friends whose parents were poor or out of work. He would buy two big loaves of bread, lunch meat, tomatoes, mayonnaise, and cake from the grocery store. That was enough to feed ten kids.

At night, if Willie had his friends over to play after school, Ernestine and Sarah would ask the kids to stay and eat dinner with the family. Willie loved the girls for what they did for him and his father, and he came to call them Aunt Ernestine and Aunt Sarah.

William Mays left the steel mill job for a better paying position with a railroad company. He didn't get to see Willie enough when he worked for the railroad company, so Mr. Mays returned to his job at the steel mill in Westfield. He earned less money than he did at the train company, but he had more time to spend with his son.

In the past, workers at steel mills in the United States were required to live in company-owned housing and shop at company-owned stores.

The steel mill owned the house that William, Willie, Sarah, and Ernestine lived in. Nearly everything in the town of Westfield was owned by the steel mill. Instead of paying workers in money, the steel mill paid workers in chits. Workers used these small pieces of paper to purchase food, clothing, and other items from stores that were run by the steel mill. Steel workers were forced to buy everything they needed from the company, and the company had a great deal of control over the people who lived in Westfield.

Willie Mays said he was always surrounded by baseball and that he always enjoyed the game. His father never forced him into it. That's what made it so easy for Willie. He didn't feel like he had to do it to make his father proud. His father let Willie choose baseball for himself, and that took off a lot of the pressure. Mr. Mays hoped his son would become a professional baseball player, but he didn't force it. William Mays said baseball had to be something Willie wanted for himself. But Willie did want to play the game, and that made his father happy.

Willie's fascination with baseball grew even stronger when he found out that his father was actually paid to play! Thinking back to the time when he learned that men could be paid to play a game they loved, Willie says in his autobiography, *Say Hey*, "That seemed to me just about the nicest idea anyone ever thought up."

Willie was so eager to play ball that he rushed out of school ready to play every day. Willie and his friends played in the field where they ate lunch. Running to the field after school, they split up into teams and played for the fun of it.

They didn't have expensive baseball equipment. Sometimes they didn't have *any* equipment. But they played anyway.

For instance, they didn't have a real baseball bat. They had no catcher's mask or chest protector, and no helmets. Hardly any of the kids even had baseball gloves!

They used a stick for a bat, and for a ball they used whatever they could find. Willie was usually one of the first kids picked in those

As a kid, Willie often had to improvise equipment for a baseball game. It was common for young baseball fans of his era to play stickball on city streets.

afternoon games. Even when the older kids took over the field, they let Willie hang around to play because he was just so good. He could run, throw, hit, and catch as well as any boy in town.

Besides being a good athlete, Willie had great eyesight. He had a wide range of vision. That meant he could see things other people couldn't. He noticed things out of the corner of his eye that most people didn't.

Mr. Mays was able to put away some of the money he made at the railroad company. And when he went back to work at the steel mill, he took a part-time job so he could save more. Mr. Mays wanted to buy a new house for his family so he could stop paying rent to the steel mill. By the time Willie was ten years old, his family had saved enough money to move out of the steel company house and into a house of their own outside of Westfield, in Fairfield, Alabama. It was a small cottage with a small front lawn, a big front porch, and a nice backyard. It wasn't a large house, but Mr. Mays owned it.

Willie liked his new neighborhood and school. He made friends with a boy named Charlie Willis who lived nearby. The boys became best friends, and they spent most of their time together. Both of them loved sports, movies, and comic books. They both loved baseball, and they played catch as they walked to school together. They traded comic books, went to the movies, and listened to the radio together. When they weren't playing baseball or football outside, they were inside playing. They were like brothers.

Willie nicknamed Charlie "Cool," and Charlie called Willie "Buck." The nicknames stayed with them as they grew up, but no one called Willie by the name of Buck when he got into the major leagues. They called him "Say Hey." Buck was a name used only by people who knew Willie as a boy in Westfield.

When he was twelve years old, Willie climbed a tree so he could watch a football game. He didn't have enough money to get into the stadium. Unfortunately, Willie fell out of the tree and broke his right arm.

At first, Willie didn't even realize his arm was broken. He was more worried that if he complained, the other kids would make fun of him, so he tried to brush it off. He ignored the pain and ran home.

Willie was also scared that his dad would punish him for climbing the tree because that was something his dad had told him not to do. But eventually the pain got so bad that Willie couldn't hide it anymore. He broke down and told his dad.

But Willie didn't get in trouble. His father took him to a doctor to get his arm checked out.

When his arm healed, it seemed like it was stronger than before. Willie had thrown underhanded before he had broken his arm. After it healed, Willie said it was more comfortable to throw overhand. His throws were even more powerful and more accurate!

One day, when Willie was playing baseball with his friends in Fairfield, he received his first offer to play ball for a semiprofessional team. It was with the Fairfield Gray Sox. The other players on the team were at least fifteen years old. Willie was only thirteen at the time, but he was just as good as the older kids.

Willie played shortstop at first, but when he fielded the ball, he threw it so hard to first base that the first baseman complained to the coach. Willie remembers what the coach said to him: "Willie, I think your arm's too good to waste at shortstop. I want you to pitch our next game."

Willie was thrilled! The pitcher was involved in every play of the game. The pitcher got all the attention and was usually the best athlete on the team. The crowds cheered for Willie when he pitched. For the first time he experienced what it was like to be a star. Willie's fastball was too much for the opposing team. They couldn't hit it. He was so excited after the game that he ran home to tell his father all about it.

Mr. Mays was happy for his son, but he worried that a pitcher's career was dangerous. If a pitcher hurt his arm, it was all over. He wouldn't be able to play any more. If a young player could learn to hit the ball and play the field, he would still have a career if his arm gave out.

When Willie finished telling his dad about winning the game, Mr. Mays said he was proud of Willie. Then he asked Willie to stop pitching. Willie was upset at first, but he understood when his father explained to him that a ballplayer had a better chance at a successful career if he learned to hit and play the field.

His father said to him, "If a pitcher hurts his arm, he's finished in baseball, unless he knows how to play the whole game. Now, most pitchers never bother to learn anything but pitching. I don't want that to happen to you. You've got to work on hitting, fielding, throwing—everything. Maybe you will be a pitcher someday, maybe not. But whatever you are, you'll be a complete ballplayer. I don't want you to waste your whole future by trying to be a star at thirteen."

Willie was let down, but he listened to his dad. He was aware that his father knew a lot about how the game of baseball should be played. So Willie kept working on his hitting, running, and fielding skills.

He found out that his father was right. Willie reached the major leagues in 1951 and played there as a center fielder for twenty-three years. Getting to the major leagues wasn't even Willie's biggest accomplishment. Willie outright dominated the major leagues for fifteen of those years.

Many Americans lost everything in the stock market crash of October 1929.
The entire nation was impoverished for more than a decade afterward.

The Depression, Discrimination, and the Negro Leagues

Times were tough when Willie was growing up. He was born in 1931, near the beginning of the Great Depression. The Great Depression was sparked by the disastrous stock market crash of Thursday, October 24, 1929. People call this day Black Thursday.

Before the crash, many Americans were doing very well financially. They earned and spent lots of money in the 1920s and invested lots of money in the stock market. Investing in the stock market is a lot like gambling. It can be dangerous.

When people invest in the stock market, they buy shares of stock. A share of stock is like a piece of a company. If the company does well and makes money, it becomes more valuable. When a company becomes more valuable, more people want to own a piece of it and more people buy shares in it. When people buy shares of stock, its value goes up. When the value goes up, everyone who owns the stock makes money.

Companies were doing so well in the 1920s that people started buying on margin. This was like buying things with a credit card. It enabled people to get what they wanted right away, as long as they promised to pay it off over time. Buying on margin allowed people who didn't have much money to buy pieces of companies they thought would do well. But at the end of the 1920s, people began to notice that all the buying of stocks in companies had inflated the values of these companies. People realized that the value of their shares was less than what they had paid for them.

People started selling away the shares they had bought. They wanted to get rid of them before the value of the shares fell even more.

When many people sell shares of stock at the same time, the value of the stock goes down a lot. This makes other shareholders very nervous. Then there is a huge rush to sell stock, and stock prices fall drastically. When the value of a share drops, so does the value of the company it represents. By the end of Black Thursday—a single day—companies had lost $4 billion. By the end of 1929, companies had lost $12 billion.

Many people had offered their homes or future wages as a promise to the banks that gave them money to buy stock. When the stock market crashed, many companies went broke. They laid off the people who worked for them because they couldn't afford to pay employees' wages. People who couldn't pay their debts lost their homes, their money, and their jobs.

Banks had invested money in the stock market, too. When it crashed, banks also lost a lot of money. The banks were unable to return money to the people who had opened savings accounts. So people lost their savings, too.

Out of work and out of money, many people had a hard time putting food on their tables during the Great Depression. When churches, homeless shelters, and other charitable organizations began to give away food, people hoping to get something to eat stood in long lines that snaked around entire blocks.

When Willie bought lunch for his friends in Westfield, they really appreciated it. He never realized how much it meant to them. Willie never thought his family was poor. He always had food to eat, clean clothes, and a decent pair of shoes.

Instead of having to find work when he was a teenager, Willie could spend more time playing baseball because his father and Ernestine worked at extra jobs. Everyone in Willie's life put in double duty to take care of him.

Willie never had to think about money because his family shielded him from it. But they may have protected him too much. When Willie got older, he struggled with money. Although he made $100,000 a year, there was a time when he had nothing to show for it. Willie had been the highest paid player in all of baseball, but he hadn't spent his money wisely. When it came to finances, he needed other people to advise him.

Discrimination and Racism

Discrimination is still a problem in this country, but it was a lot worse when Willie was growing up. When he was a kid, racism in America

In 1867, the National Association of Base Ball Players Nominating Committee (NABBP) drew baseball's color line. This is what the NABBP said: "It is not presumed by your Committee that any clubs who have applied are composed of persons of color, or any portion of them; and the recommendation of your Committee in this report are based upon this view, and they unanimously report against the admission of any club which may be composed of one or more colored persons." This banned any African American from playing major league baseball. The ban lasted eighty years.

prevented African Americans from playing in major league baseball.

The Emancipation Proclamation in 1863 freed people from slavery and said African Americans should be regarded and treated as equal to whites, but white Americans were slow to accept this. Jim Crow laws in the South kept blacks and whites segregated. The term "separate but equal" was used to justify this idea, and it led to the enforcement of laws that kept people apart throughout the United States.

African Americans were not allowed to eat in the same restaurants, drink from the same water fountains, or use the same bathrooms as whites. They were forced to ride in the backs of buses, and they were told to give up their seats whenever a white person came aboard.

Stores and facilities were separate, but they were not equal. African Americans earned less money, and their restaurants and stores reflected this sad fact. To this day, America is still trying to erase the color line that was created by slavery, which unfairly caused a lot of pain, humiliation, and anger for so many people.

Major league baseball teams in the North couldn't hire African American ballplayers. African American teams were prevented from playing in the major leagues. In the South, things were even worse. Near the beginning of the 1900s, Georgia passed laws forbidding blacks and whites from playing baseball within two blocks of each other. This law not only said blacks and whites couldn't play together, it said they couldn't play anywhere near each other!

According to the Interpretive Staff of the Martin Luther King Jr. National Historic Site, the state of Georgia, in the late 1800s and early 1900s, passed legislation that said, "It shall be unlawful for any amateur white baseball team to play baseball on any vacant lot or baseball diamond within two blocks of a playground devoted to the Negro race, and it shall be unlawful for any amateur colored baseball team to play baseball in any vacant lot or baseball diamond within two blocks of any playground devoted to the white race."

This prevented black and white players from getting to know each other or having equal opportunities.

In 1867, the National Association of Base Ball Players Nominating Committee (NABBP) officially drew baseball's color line by banning African Americans from the major leagues. The NABBP eventually went under, but its successor, the National Association of Professional Base Ball Players, upheld baseball's racist philosophy with an unwritten rule that barred African Americans from its teams and leagues.

This racist exclusion brought the Negro leagues into existence. Lasting until the end of the 1940s, the Negro leagues began to decline after Jackie Robinson, the first black player in the majors, was signed by the Brooklyn Dodgers.

It was pure ignorance. Baseball's organizations used racist excuses to exclude African Americans. They said that they weren't smart or that they didn't have the talent to succeed in the major leagues. This was completely wrong! When the color line was finally broken, players like Willie Mays and Jackie Robinson showed the world how wrong those claims had been.

Mays and Robinson were not only good baseball players, they were great players. They were legendary. They were better than most white ballplayers.

But before the late 1940s, none of that mattered. In 1900, there were five all-black professional teams: the Cuban Giants, whose home city varied from year to year; the Cuban X Giants; the Norfolk, Virginia, Red Stockings; the Chicago Unions; and the Chicago Colombian Giants. African American teams

The United States prohibited African Americans from living as equals until just a few decades ago. Here, a police officer enforces laws that kept black people and white people apart.

flourished in the North and Midwest. By 1906, nine Negro teams had surfaced within 100 miles of Philadelphia.

In 1910, there was an effort to establish a Negro league that included teams from all over the country—from Chicago, Louisville, New Orleans, St. Louis, Kansas City, and Columbus. African American baseball leaders said they would pay up to $300 apiece for a franchise in the league.

But the attempt failed before the league could play its first game. It would take another ten years before the first strong Negro league was established.

When the Negro leagues flourished in the 1920s and 1930s, they gave African American men the only chance they had at that time to play professional baseball. People who attended Negro league games quickly found out that the level of play was top-notch.

In 1946, when Willie was fifteen years old, major league baseball owners were discussing the idea of breaking the color line. At the time, Willie was playing with his father in the Industrial

League for the Fairfield Gray Sox. Willie played center field while his father played left field.

Willie was earning about $100 a month playing for the Gray Sox. This was great money for a high school student. Most of his friends were earning between $32 and $40 a month.

One day, a man named Lorenzo "Piper" Davis saw Willie play. Davis and Mr. Mays were good friends. Davis asked Willie if he was playing for money. Willie told him he was, and Davis said, "If you want to play for more money, have your daddy call me."

Willie went home that day and waited for his dad to get back from work. When his father got home, he called Piper Davis. Davis wanted Willie to come down to the Birmingham Black Barons' home field to try out for the team.

Mr. Mays took his son to meet with Davis, who was a coach for the Birmingham Black Barons, a professional team in the Negro National League. Davis gave Willie his first shot at professional baseball when Willie was only sixteen years old—when he was still in high school.

Willie was a good hitter at the time, but he still wasn't a professional hitter. He could hit a fastball over the fence, but he was hopeless against the curveball. Curveballs were tough for Willie because he didn't have any experience with them. Hardly any high school kids or semipro pitchers knew how to throw them. But Piper Davis believed in Willie. Davis and the Black Barons coaching staff taught Willie how to recognize a curveball when it came out of the pitcher's hand.

Good hitters can usually tell when a curveball is coming if they pay close attention to the ball as the pitcher releases it. They can recognize curveballs by watching the rotation of the ball. This is important because curveballs are a lot slower than fastballs. Also, good curveballs drop several inches before they reach home plate

A batter who mistakenly thinks he is swinging at a fastball will usually swing too soon and miss a curveball. Even if a batter manages to hit a curveball, too often it ends up as a weak ground ball or an infield pop-up.

Once Willie learned to recognize a rotating curveball, he was able to wait a little bit longer before swinging the bat. He was also able to predict how the ball would drop, and he changed his swing so he could hit it. After a few months of practice, Willie was able to hit curveballs for home runs.

Negro league baseball was very different from major league baseball. Players didn't make much money. They didn't have private planes to whisk them from city to city. They rode buses and sometimes an entire team was stuffed into a car or truck.

Especially in the South, it was often hard for a Negro league team to find a restaurant that would serve them. Teams had trouble finding hotels that would let African Americans spend the night. They often had trouble finding fields to play on because white baseball teams always got first choice.

Despite the problems, Willie enjoyed his days in the Negro leagues. He loved the game and had fun playing, no matter what the conditions were. Playing for the Black Barons

Willie's hard work as a ballplayer in the Negro National League paid off when he made it to the major leagues. Here, he makes the 3,000th hit of his career.

gave Willie the experience he needed to succeed in the major leagues. He felt the Black Barons were a better team than most major league baseball teams. When Willie finally broke into the major leagues in 1951, he thought it was actually easier to play there than in the Negro National League.

Breaking into the Big Show

In 1947, when Willie was sixteen years old, he was playing for the Black Barons. That was the year Jackie Robinson broke into the major leagues. Robinson wasn't the first African American to play on a white baseball team, but he was the first African American ballplayer to make the starting lineup of a white team in over fifty years.

White America was learning about Robinson for the first time, but Willie and many other black ballplayers already knew him. There was a lot of excitement in the air. African American ballplayers were starting to realize that they might get the chance to prove to America that they could hit, run, throw, and catch better than a lot of white ballplayers. There was a lot of pride involved.

Willie hadn't met Jackie Robinson yet, but every black ballplayer knew about Robinson and knew he symbolized opportunity.

Willie never looked at Robinson as an idol—Willie's dad was Willie's idol—but Robinson paved the way for other black ballplayers to break into major league baseball. Willie looked up to him for this. Most black ballplayers saw Robinson as a symbol of opportunity and acceptance. Robinson also absorbed a lot of hatred. Many white fans and players in the major leagues were incredibly racist, and Robinson heard about it over and over from them.

Willie's entrance into the major leagues came as an accident. Eddie Montague was a scout from the New York Giants, a successful National League baseball team. Montague was sent to Birmingham to look at Alonzo Perry, one of Willie's teammates on the Black Barons. But after watching the Black Barons game, Montague was interested in Willie. He could see during the game that Willie was incredibly talented.

In 1947, Jackie Robinson became the first African American to play in the modern major leagues, breaking the color barrier that had existed since the late 1800s.

Montague tracked Willie down and approached him one day as he was getting off the Black Barons' bus. This is how Willie describes the conversation in *Say Hey*:

Montague asked, "Would you like to play professional baseball, Willie?"

"Yes sir!" Willie could hardly believe what he was hearing.

"Would you like to play for the Giants?"

"Yes, sir," Willie said.

"I'll talk to Mr. Hayes about it then."

Tom Hayes was the owner of the Black Barons.

Willie had a good game that day. He hit three doubles and made some great plays in the outfield. After the game, Montague took Willie aside to talk.

"Everything's okay with Mr. Hayes. I saw him during the game and I'm going to talk to him about your contract," Montague said.

"What contract?" Willie had never signed a contract with the Black Barons.

"Didn't you sign a contract with him?" Montague asked.

"No, sir. I didn't sign any contract with him. I just told him I'd play."

"Whom should I talk to then?

"My father and Aunt Sarah."

The next night, Willie and his father signed a contract with Sioux City, a minor league team owned by the New York Giants. Willie's father had to sign the contract because Willie was a minor and still too young. Willie got a $4,000 signing bonus and a salary of $250 a month. The year was 1950.

This was a huge step in the right direction, but Willie never got to play for Sioux City. Racial discrimination kept him out of the team's lineup. The city had been torn apart by racism when a Native American was buried in an all-white cemetery.

This happened just a few days before Willie was signed, and Sioux City did not want to take Willie. The team feared that having an African American ballplayer would reflect badly upon them. Willie was surprised by this. He had never really felt discrimination, but then he had never played outside the Negro leagues.

Despite the racism of the era, even white fans grew to love the talented
Willie Mays.

Despite having played only half the season, Willie led the league's outfielders in assists. An outfielder is credited with an assist when he picks up or catches the ball and throws out a runner at one of the bases in the infield. Willie's strong arm and sharp fielding skills were starting to get noticed.

Chick Genovese, the manager of the Trenton Giants, thought Willie was the best ballplayer he had ever seen. And he had seen lots of ballplayers. Genovese told New York Giants manager Leo Durocher about Willie's talents.

A Rising Star

*"Hey kid, what are you
going to show me today?"*

These were the first words Leo Durocher ever said to Willie, as reported in *Say Hey*. It was in the spring of 1951. Willie had shown the Giants that he was a great ballplayer in 1950, and they rewarded him. They moved him from the Class B Trenton Giants to the Minneapolis Millers. The Millers were a Class AAA team. AAA is the highest level in minor league baseball. There is only one level above it—the major leagues.

"I've got quite a report on you from Trenton, kid. This guy Chick Genovese thinks you're the greatest he ever saw," Durocher said.

"Oh, really. What did the report say?" Willie asked.

"It said that your hat keeps flying off."

Willie realized after a while that the fans loved it when his hat fell off. It looked like he was running so fast that he ran right out from under the hat. After Willie got to the major leagues, he started wearing a hat that was one size too big so it would fall off more often. He did this to entertain the fans.

Willie felt like the jump from B ball to AAA ball was just as important as the jump from the Negro leagues into the major leagues. He and other black players on the team were still dealing with racial discrimination, but they were so happy for the opportunity they had been given that they worked hard not let it affect them.

Before the start of the 1951 season, Tommy Heath, the Millers' manager, told Willie that he'd probably be called up to the big show—the major leagues—before the end of the season.

That same year, Ray Dandridge, one of the best players ever to play in the Negro leagues, spoke to Willie. As reported in *Say Hey*, this is what Dandridge said:

This photo of Willie was taken on May 25, 1951, just before he played his first major league game with the New York Giants.

"You got a great chance. When I played in the black leagues, we were barnstorming most of the time. Sometimes I played three games in one day. We made about $35 a week and ate hamburgers. You're going to eat steak and you're going to make a lot of money. You just keep it clean and be a good boy."

The encouragement Willie got from Heath and Dandridge gave Willie even more of an incentive to play as hard as he could.

On opening day of the 1951 season, Willie woke up and saw snow falling. This was crazy. Baseball begins in the spring. It was only the second time Willie had seen snow. How could there be a baseball game in the snow?

Willie went back to sleep, but a phone call from Tommy Heath woke him. Heath had ordered a helicopter to blow the snow off the field. Willie played and got a few hits. By the end of the season's first week, he was batting .477.

The Millers began the season on the road, playing on other teams' ball fields. Willie played very well during the opening road trip.

His playing was so good that people in Minneapolis had a hard time believing what they read in the newspapers. According to *Say Hey*, one sportswriter told Willie that editors at his newspaper had told him to "tone it down." They wanted him to write more objective stories. By the time the Millers returned home to Minneapolis, the fans expected great things from Willie.

Willie gave them what they wanted. In the Millers' first home stand at Nicollet Park, Willie knocked the leather off the baseball. During the sixteen-game stretch, Willie came up to the plate sixty-three times and had thirty-eight hits. He batted .608! He batted in fifteen runs. There was only one game during that period when he didn't get a hit. Willie was playing at an incredible pace.

Willie made his mark in the field as well as on the base paths. He stole six bases during the home stand. He made an incredible play when he climbed the center field fence, jumped and caught a deep line drive off the bat of a slugger named Taft Wright.

Willie leaps high off the ground to make a spectacular catch off a line drive near the top of the outfield wall.

Taft couldn't believe Willie had caught the ball. Literally. As reported in *Say Hey*, Taft slid into second base, dusted himself off, and started arguing when the umpire said, "You're out."

"No I'm not," Taft said. "He didn't catch that. He couldn't." Taft stayed on the field screaming at the umpire, and he had to be taken off by his coach.

In thirty-five games with Minneapolis that year, Willie hit .477 with eight home runs and thirty runs batted in (RBIs). He scored thirty-eight runs and had a total of seventy-one hits, including three triples and thirty-five doubles.

Ballplayers who put up these kind of numbers don't stay in AAA for long, especially when they're only twenty years old.

Willie was in Sioux City when he got the call. He was doing what he enjoyed most after baseball—seeing a movie on his day off. About halfway through the picture, an usher came into the theater. The lights came on, and the usher got up on stage to make an announcement.

"If Willie Mays is in the audience, would he please report to his manager at the hotel?"

Willie got scared at first. He was afraid something had happened to his father or someone else back home. He rushed back to the hotel and found his coach. The coach said he had just gotten off the telephone with the New York Giants. They wanted Willie to play for their major league team!

The Giants already had great outfielders, including Hall of Famer Bobby Thomson. Willie wondered how he'd break into the lineup and worried that he wouldn't get any playing time.

When Willie came to the Giants in 1951, he joined a team that was in transition. The team, who had hit 221 home runs in 1947, was full of sluggers. But none of the sluggers could run. Bill Rigney led the team with just seven stolen bases.

Leo Durocher was hired as the Giants' manager in 1948, and he wanted to build a more balanced team. Instead of loading the lineup with slow sluggers, Durocher wanted to put a speedy team on the field. Willie had power and speed, and that's why he was such an important part of Durocher's plan.

As the manager of the New York Giants, Leo "the Lip" Durocher served as a mentor to Willie. Durocher is said to have coined the phrase "Nice guys finish last."

Willie ended up looking toward Durocher as another uncle, giving him a lot of credit for bringing him into the majors. Durocher had patience with Willie and tried to make him feel comfortable. Willie never forgot this, and he has always spoken very highly of Durocher.

Durocher realized Willie would be nervous when he came to the majors, so he tried to make him feel at home. Durocher told Willie that he had faith in his ability to become a star.

As Willie got dressed in the locker room before his first major league game, Durocher told him he'd be playing center field and batting third. Willie was shocked. In baseball, a team's best all-around athlete plays center field. Furthermore, a team's best hitter almost always bats third.

This is because the third batter in the lineup has the best odds of coming to the plate with runners on base. The manager wants the best hitter at bat when there are players in scoring position.

Willie tried to stay calm, but his heart was racing. He was still getting over the shock of playing in the major leagues. Now he was in the starting lineup and playing center field.

Willie's fear showed when he stepped onto the field. He went 0 for 5 in his first major league game. Willie was 0 for 3 in his second game, and 0 for 4 in his third game. Willie had just one hit in his first twenty-five major league at bats. He was crushed.

One day, after another hitless game, Durocher found Willie sitting near his locker. Willie was crying. Willie told Durocher he couldn't hit in the majors.

"The pitching is just too fast for me here. They're going to send me back to Minneapolis," he said, according to *Say Hey*.

After his first twenty-five games in the majors, Willie had begun to question his ability. Major league pitchers were much better than the pitchers he had been facing in AAA. Struggling at the plate, Willie wondered why he had even been brought to the majors. Willie was in a slump.

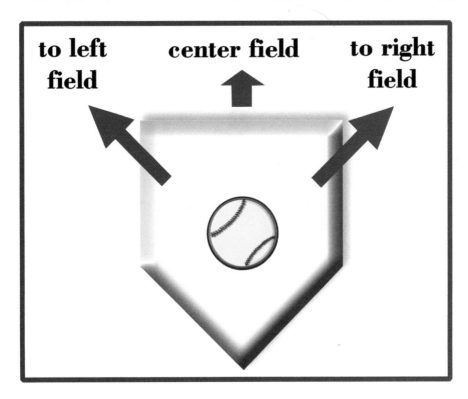

to left field center field to right field

Willie had a problem that is common among hitters: because he was right-handed, he tended to hit the ball into left field. When a batter pulls the ball, he makes it easier for fielders to anticipate where the ball will go, so they are more likely to catch it.

Durocher told Willie that he was having problems hitting because he was trying to pull everything. Willie was a right-handed hitter, and he was trying to pull the ball into left field.

Durocher explained that right-handed hitters almost always struggle when they try to pull, or hit, every pitch into left field—especially when they try to pull pitches on the outside part of the plate.

Durocher taught Willie how to hit the ball where it is pitched. For example, if the ball came in from the right, he would try to hit it toward right field.

To hit the ball hard, a batter should hit the ball where it's pitched. When a hitter sees a pitch on the right side of the plate, he should hit it to right field. When the ball is on the left side of the plate, he should hit to left field. The same method would apply to a pitch in the middle of the plate. A hitter should smack it into center field.

When hitters go against this simple philosophy, they tend to hit weak ground balls or pop-ups, or they strike out. Once Durocher explained this to Willie, things started to change.

After sinking into that 1 for 25 slump, Willie started to hit the ball. He went 2 for 3 in his next game, and 9 for 24 over the next stretch of games.

Once he started getting hits, Willie began to believe in himself again. Durocher's advice was paying off. Eventually Willie felt that he could get a hit every time he stepped into the batter's box.

Willie and the Giants started to play good baseball that year, but they were still way behind the Dodgers in the National League East division. Halfway through the season, they trailed the Dodgers by thirteen games.

The Dodgers were playing great ball. This upset the Giants because the two teams were cross-town rivals. The Dodgers played at Ebbets Field in New York City's borough of Brooklyn. The Giants played at the Polo Grounds in the borough of Manhattan. Their stadiums were only about a twenty-minute subway ride from each other. New York City baseball fans were paying close attention, and the Giants didn't want to embarrass themselves.

Just after the all-star break, which is the halfway point of the major league's season, the Giants swept the Dodgers, winning each game in a four-game set. The Giants went on a sixteen-game winning streak and crept up in the rankings. By September, Willie Mays's Giants were just five games behind Jackie Robinson's Dodgers.

It's still hard to believe how that 1951 season ended. At the beginning of the year, Willie thought the Giants had no chance of catching the Dodgers. Probably everyone else did, too. They were wrong.

The Giants surprised everyone as they won thirty-seven out of forty-four games down the stretch. With one game left to play, the teams were tied for first place! They had both won ninety-six games.

Willie went 0 for 4 in the last game of the season, but the Giants beat the Boston Braves. Thanks to Jackie Robinson, the Dodgers beat the Philadelphia Phillies, too. Robinson hurt himself on a game-saving play in the twelfth inning, then hit a game-winning home run in the fourteenth!

This made New York City the center of the baseball world. Baseball fans were going crazy. Willie's Giants and Jackie's Dodgers had stolen the spotlight from the New York Yankees, who had won the World Series in 1949 and 1950.

The Yankees finished first in the American League that year and were preparing to go for a third consecutive World Series title. But on the last day of the 1951 season, no one was talking about the Yankees. New York baseball fans were getting ready for a three-game playoff series between the Giants and Dodgers. The outcome would decide who owned New York— Manhattan's Giants or Brooklyn's Dodgers. In Willie's first year ever in the majors, he had a chance to get to the World Series!

Willie went 0 for 3 and struck out twice in the first game, but the Giants won it 3–1. In the second game, Willie's Giants were blown away by the Dodgers and shut out 0–10.

The teams split the first two games of the series, so it all came down to a single game. The winner would play the New York Yankees in the World Series.

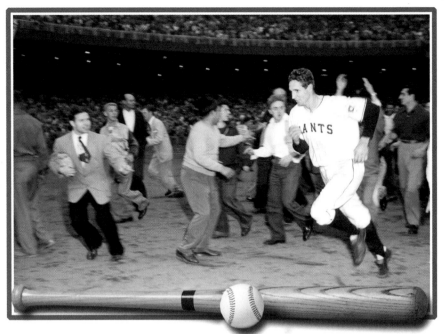

Bobby Thomson's home run in the bottom of the ninth sent the Giants to the World Series in 1951, and is still considered one of the greatest moments in baseball history.

In the Giants' biggest game of the season, Willie went 0 for 3 with a strikeout. The Giants came to bat in the bottom of the ninth, down by a score of 1–4. But the Giants mounted a dramatic comeback in the ninth inning. With bases loaded, Bobby Thomson crushed a fastball over the left field fence to give the Giants a 5–4 victory.

Thomson's home run has been seen by millions of people over the years. Baseball fans who weren't even alive when he hit it recognize it as one of the greatest sports moments ever.

The powerful words of Giants television announcer Russ Hodges have been etched in legend: "The Giants win the pennant! The Giants win the pennant!"

Willie was on deck when Thomson hit that home run. He was happy, too. His team won, and the pressure had been removed from him.

It was the highlight of the season for Willie and the Giants. They played well in the World Series, but Joe Dimaggio and Mickey Mantle were too much for the Giants. The Yankees won the 1951 World Series four games to two.

But it had been an incredible season for Willie. During his first year in the majors, he had managed a .274 batting average and had swatted twenty home runs. Willie was voted National League Rookie of the Year, the third straight African American ballplayer to be awarded this honor. Best of all, he had proved to everyone that he deserved the starting center field position that Coach Durocher had entrusted to him.

This was extremely important to the African American community. It demonstrated that dozens of ballplayers who never made it out

During his first year in the majors, Willie had a .274 batting average and hit twenty home runs. He was named National League Rookie of the Year, the third straight African American ballplayer to receive the honor.

of the Negro leagues could have succeeded in the major leagues. It highlighted how narrow-minded many Americans had been.

Before the Dodgers drafted Jackie Robinson, it had been fifty years since an African American started for a major league team. The Major League Baseball organization was starting to realize that African Americans were just as good—and sometimes better—than the white ballplayers. The early successes of Willie and Jackie paved the way for more African Americans to enter the league and thrive within it.

A few days after the 1951 World Series ended, Willie was drafted by the army. The United States was at war with Korea and needed young men to fight.

Willie played only thirty-four games with the Giants in 1952. Before he left for the army, the Giants had a 26–8 record. They were the best team in baseball. Once he was gone, the team fell apart. In 1952, the Giants finished second to the Dodgers.

Willie didn't get to play a single game for the Giants in 1953, but he did learn his famous basket catch technique. He spent his time in the army as a baseball instructor. While he was there, another soldier showed him that if he held his glove near his chest when he caught the ball, he'd be in a better position to throw it. Willie practiced the technique and revealed it to the world in 1954 when he made what might be the greatest catch in the history of baseball.

Willie was drafted into the army to fight in Korea, but spent most of his time in the service teaching baseball. It was there that he learned his now-famous basket catch.

At the start of the 1954 season, Giants manager Leo Durocher told New York sportswriters that Willie would hit .300 with thirty home runs. It was a pretty risky prediction. Willie hit well in exhibition games that spring, but he hadn't faced major league pitching in almost two years and people thought he might be rusty.

People had a hard time believing Durocher. While Willie was in the army, the Dodgers' Duke Snider and the Yankees' Mickey Mantle were the best center fielders in the league. No one mentioned Willie Mays when they talked about New York's great center fielders. But Durocher's prediction proved to be true.

Willie had an incredible year. In 1954, his first full season in the majors, Willie led the National League with an incredible .345 batting average. He led the league in triples (thirteen) and in slugging percentage (.667). And he had slammed forty-one home runs.

The Giants won the pennant with ninety-seven victories that year. They owned New York City now. Neither the Yankees nor the Dodgers had made the playoffs.

The Giants were set to play the Cleveland Indians in the World Series. The Indians had played legendary ball that year, having won 111 games. Seeming unstoppable, they were favored to win the World Series. None of that mattered, though. The Giants overpowered the Indians and swept the 1954 World Series.

Willie's over-the-shoulder basket catch in the eighth inning of Game 1 set the tone for the World Series. To make it, he had raced toward the center field fence and caught a line drive that would have landed about 430 or 440 feet away from home plate.

If Willie hadn't made that catch, the Giants probably would have lost the game. There's no telling what would have happened then!

The catch has been played on television thousands of times through the years. Because it was a very important play in the World Series, people say it was the best catch ever made. Willie didn't think so. He always felt he had made better catches, but the World Series basket catch is the one everyone remembers.

A Baseball Legend

Willie made the game look easy. Incredibly graceful, he was a pleasure to watch. Besides his natural ability, he had a magnetic personality. Sportswriters and fans warmed up to him. Besides loving to watch him play, people respected him as a person off the field.

By the time the 1954 World Series was over, Willie was at the center of every baseball discussion. He won the Most Valuable Player award, the most prestigious award a ballplayer can earn. It means that he did more for his team than any other player in the entire league. It was the first of two MVP honors for Willie. He won it again in 1965, when he hit fifty-two home runs.

Year	G	AB	R	H	2B	3B	HR	RBI	BB	SO	SB	CS	AVG	OBP	SLG
1951	121	464	59	127	22	5	20	68	57	60	7	4	.274	.356	.472
1952	34	127	17	30	2	4	4	23	16	17	4	1	.236	.326	.409
1954	151	565	119	195	33	13	41	110	66	57	8	5	.345	.415	.667
1955	152	580	123	185	18	13	51	127	79	60	24	4	.319	.404	.659
1956	152	578	101	171	27	8	36	84	68	65	40	10	.296	.371	.557
1957	152	585	112	195	26	20	35	97	76	62	38	19	.333	.411	.626
1958	152	600	121	208	33	11	29	96	78	56	31	6	.347	.423	.583
1959	151	575	125	180	43	5	34	104	65	58	27	4	.313	.385	.583
1960	153	595	107	190	29	12	29	103	61	70	25	10	.319	.386	.555
1961	154	572	129	176	32	3	40	123	81	77	18	9	.308	.395	.584
1962	162	621	130	189	36	5	49	141	78	85	18	2	.304	.385	.615
1963	157	596	115	187	32	7	38	103	66	83	8	3	.314	.384	.582
1964	157	578	121	171	21	9	47	111	82	72	19	5	.296	.384	.607
1965	157	558	118	177	21	3	52	112	76	71	9	4	.317	.399	.645
1966	152	552	99	159	29	4	37	103	70	81	5	1	.288	.370	.556
1967	141	486	83	128	22	2	22	70	51	92	6	0	.263	.336	.453
1968	148	498	84	144	20	5	23	79	67	81	12	6	.289	.376	.488
1969	117	403	64	114	17	3	13	58	49	71	6	2	.283	.365	.437
1970	139	478	94	139	15	2	28	83	79	90	5	0	.291	.395	.506
1971	136	417	82	113	24	5	18	61	112	123	23	3	.271	.429	.482
1972	88	244	35	61	11	1	8	22	60	48	4	5	.250	.400	.402
1973	66	209	24	44	10	0	6	25	27	47	1	0	.211	.304	.344

KEY: g = games, ab = at bats, r = runs, h = hits, 2b = doubles, 3b = triples, hr = home runs, rbi = runs batted in, bb = walks, so = strikeouts, sb = stolen bases, cs = caught stealing, avg = batting average, obp = on base percentage, slg = slugging average

These are the career statistics of Willie Mays. He had one of the best careers of any ballplayer in the history of the game.

Willie's enthusiasm, charisma, and athletic ability earned him the nickname "the Say Hey Kid." Willie had become a celebrity. It was impossible to talk about New York's great center fielders without talking about Willie Mays. Recording artists even wrote songs about Willie.

Baseball fans and sportswriters started wondering who was better—Mickey Mantle or Willie Mays. Mantle had more power. He could hit longer home runs, but Willie hit more of them. Most people agreed that Willie was faster and that he was a better center fielder. Over the years, Willie has won the battle. Most people admit that Mays was better than Mantle, and maybe the best ever.

Willie Mays's Career Totals	
Games:	2,992
At bats:	10,881
Runs:	2,062
Hits:	3,283
Doubles:	523
Triples:	140
Home runs:	660
Runs batted in:	1,903
Walks:	1,464
Strikeouts:	1,526
Stolen bases:	338
Caught stealing:	103
Batting average:	.302
On base percentage:	.387
Slugging percentage:	.557

Willie is third on the all-time home run list. His 660 career home runs put him right behind Hank Aaron and Babe Ruth. Mantle won more MVP awards, but there was more competition in the National League. The National League had

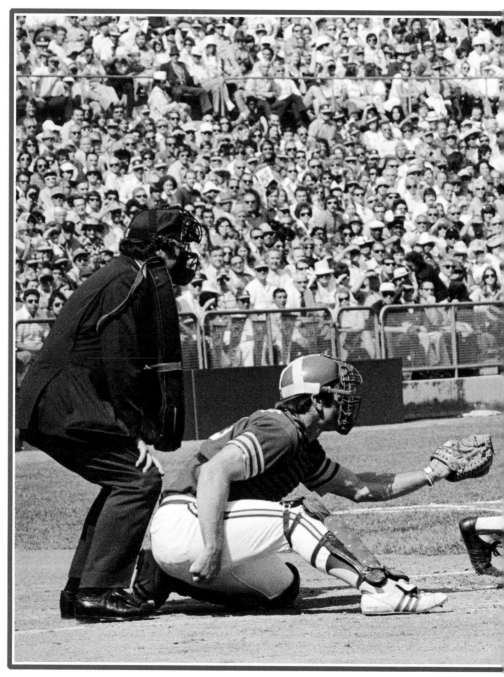

Willie gets the first hit of the 1973 World Series as an outfielder for the New York Mets. He retired after the series.

better players in the 1950s. There wasn't much doubt about who the best player was in the American League. It was Mickey Mantle.

But the National League featured several outstanding players during the late 1950s and early 1960s. In addition to Willie Mays, fans could enjoy watching Hank Aaron, Frank Robinson, Ernie Banks, Eddie Mathews, Warren Spahn, and Sandy Koufax. All of these players are in Major League Baseball's Hall of Fame.

Mays's best traits were probably his confidence and enthusiasm. Whereas Mickey Mantle didn't seem to enjoy playing the game and was hard on himself, Willie enjoyed every game he played. He played baseball for the love of it.

Willie said during his career that he would have played for whatever money the Giants were willing to pay. The money he earned was an added bonus. It seemed like a gift to him. Willie was an African American man who was raised in a poor town. He felt like his life was charmed.

Arnold Hano, who wrote many baseball books in the 1950s and 1960s, wrote a biography of Mays in 1966, called *Willie Mays*. Hano said of

Willie: "He was thought to be special, very special. Almost immediately, he became a special ballplayer. When you think of natural ballplayers, only two come into mind, Babe Ruth and Willie Mays. He probably could have played in the major leagues when he was sixteen."

His thoughts on Mickey Mantle were different. "Most people thought that Mays was the better . . . I don't know exactly what the numbers said, but there was something about Mays that always went beyond that. Even today, you don't hear about Mantle doing anything except hitting tape-measure home runs."

Hano felt that Mays's and Mantle's characters set them apart. He said, "Mantle played ball almost under a shroud of depression, because he always thought he was going to die an early death. But Mays probably thinks he's going to live forever. Mantle acted like a man who was doomed. Mays never did, even though he played long beyond his ability.

"I talked to Willie after the 1973 World Series, in which he looked terrible. I said, 'What were you doing out there, Willie?'

" 'Oh, I was having fun!' " he told me.

"Mantle never had fun. Mays, on the other hand, seemed to be inoculated from all the pressure. He simply went beyond the usual frames of reference.

"That's the way we all felt, and I think it was true for not only the press, but also for managers and other players. And this bled into the other pages of the newspaper."

Willie even said it himself: "I could never understand how some players are always talking about baseball being hard work. To me, it's always been a pleasure, even when I feel sort of draggy after a doubleheader."

Willie realized how popular he was when he went to Puerto Rico to play winter ball. When his plane landed at 6:45 in the morning, a thousand fans were there to greet him.

He played that winter with a great team, which included Roberto Clemente, who became the first Puerto Rican player to make it big in the majors. The Pittsburgh Pirates drafted Clemente and had him in the starting lineup in 1955.

Willie Mays was in Puerto Rico playing winter ball when he posed for this photo on January 15, 1955.

The Giants had no chance of catching the Dodgers in 1955, but Willie was a home run machine. He hit 51 home runs that year. Willie hit 50 home runs twice in his career. Not many other players can say that. In addition to Willie, the other big home-run hitters did it in a completely different era of baseball.

Hank Aaron is the all-time home-run king. He hit 755 home runs in his career, but he never hit 50 in a single season. When Willie hit 52 home runs in 1965, he and Babe Ruth were the only two sluggers ever to have more than one 50 home-run season.

Since the baseball strike of 1994, there have been more teams in the league. Many people say that having so many teams has thinned the talent pool. Struggling teams are forced to start rookie pitchers, and sluggers have been feasting on this.

Also, over the past ten years, baseball stadiums have gotten smaller. When Willie played at the Polo Grounds in the 1950s, the center field fence was 450 feet away from home plate. These days, the distance to the fence in

Willie is presented with the Gold Glove Award for being chosen the 1957 center fielder of the year.

straightaway center is about 400 feet. Just think about how many more home runs Willie might have hit if he had the chance to play in the smaller ballparks!

Many people think that the baseball used in the major leagues today is harder than the one that was used when Willie played. People think that these days the ball is wound tighter, that it's "juiced." This means that it travels farther when it is hit.

Willie beats a throw at home plate to score all the way from first base on a teammate's grounder.

The Say Hey Kid won two MVP awards, eleven years apart. He hit 660 home runs during his career. Willie twice hit more than 50 homers in a National League season. He once belted four homers in a single game.

There are quite a few players who have hit .300 for their careers, but Willie did it with power and longevity. He had 3,283 hits and is number 11 on the all-time list. Willie's lifetime average was .302. His 2,062 runs rank fifth on the all-time list. His 1,903 RBIs rank ninth of all time.

Odds are always against the hitter. The best hitters in all of baseball fail seven out of ten times at the plate. Even if a batter hits the ball very hard, there are nine men in the field waiting to catch the ball. The first two foul balls count as strikes, and if a fielder catches a foul ball, the batter is out.

Willie was the first player to hit 300 homers and steal 300 bases (338 total) in a career. He led the National League in steals four consecutive seasons. When on bases, his daring steals drove pitchers crazy, destroying their concentration and making it easier for the hitters who followed him in the lineup.

The Gold Glove award came into existence in 1957. It is given to the best player at each position in the major leagues. Willie earned one for each of the first twelve years he played.

He is the only outfielder with more than 7,000 career putouts. He made some of the most acrobatic catches baseball has ever seen. The Vic Wertz catch he made in Game 1 of the 1954 World Series is the most famous, but it probably wasn't his best.

Life After Baseball

When the 1963 season started, Willie began to think about life after baseball. The Giants had moved to San Francisco five years earlier. It would be ten years before he announced his retirement from the major leagues, but the idea was beginning to weigh on him.

Mays had married Marghuerite Wendell just before his twenty-fifth birthday in 1956. They remained together for seven years and adopted a baby boy, Michael, in 1958. Marghuerite divorced Willie in 1963.

Mays married his second wife, Mae Louise Allen, a social worker, in November 1971. They live in Atherton, California.

Through all this, money was tight. Willie had made bad investments in real estate and

Willie's first wife Marghuerite looks on as he signs the papers for the purchase of a new home.

restaurants. Broke, he considered filing for bankruptcy. It took a few years, but he got himself out of debt.

Willie had a very productive year in 1970, but for the most part, his age was catching up with him. In the late 1960s and early 1970s, Willie still loved the game, but he was tired. Money was part of the reason he continued to play. He had wasted money over the years. He wasn't rich.

Most fans agree that Willie played beyond his prime. Willie was traded by the Giants to the New York Mets in 1972. A story about the trade in the *New York Times* began like this:

"Willie Mays, a $165,000-a-year folk hero at the age of 41, was traded yesterday to the New York Mets by the San Francisco Giants after one of the most complex series of negotiations in baseball history. When it finally was completed, it returned Mays to the New York baseball scene where he had started his career, 21 years and 646 home runs ago."

Willie was upset. The Giants had been so secretive that he learned about the trade from a sportswriter from the *New York Daily News*.

He spent more than a year with the Mets. With his last 200 career at bats in 1973, he managed just forty hits and barely hit .200, finishing the year with six home runs.

Age had taken the speed from Willie's legs. He was able to steal only one base that year. His legs were in constant pain. He couldn't play center field anymore. The Mets coach, Yogi Berra, was forced to move Willie to first base

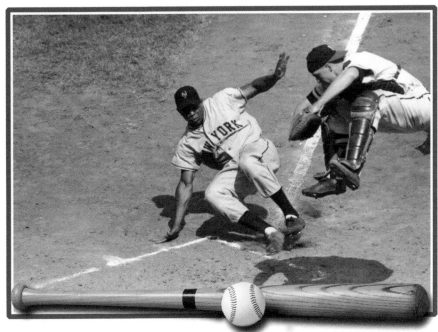

Willie slides safely into home plate beneath the legs of a catcher.

from center field. Willie's last year was a tribute to his years in New York.

On September 25, 1973, Willie announced his retirement from baseball to the fans at Shea Stadium in New York. This is part of what he said:

"In my heart, I'm a sad man. Just to hear you cheer like this for me and not be able to do anything about it makes me a very sad man. This is my farewell. You don't know what's going on inside of me tonight. Now that I have all I need, I

Willie tips his hat to fans for the last time during farewell ceremonies for him at Shea Stadium in Queens, New York, on September 26, 1973, the day after he retired from baseball.

can teach other kids to be as great an athlete as I am. If I see someone that has this talent, I will help them. I want to say hello to all my friends, and Willie, say good-bye to America."

Willie cried after giving the speech.

The Mets won the National League East division that year and got to the World Series against the Oakland Athletics. Willie didn't get much playing time in the series. The Mets lost the World Series to Oakland, four games to three.

When Willie retired, the Mets gave him a coaching job. But it was very hard for him to accept that he no longer had his youth, that he could no longer play baseball.

He would wake up in the middle of the night thinking about the game. He was a nervous wreck on the field and had to leave the stadium before games started.

In 1979, Willie was voted into the Hall of Fame the very first time his name appeared on the ballot. That has only happened a few times.

Willie gave a short speech at the ceremony. "What can I say? This country is made up of a great many things. You can grow up to be what

WILLIE HOWARD MAYS, JR.
"THE SAY HEY KID"
NEW YORK N.L., SAN FRANCISCO N.L.,
NEW YORK N.L., 1951 - 1973
ONE OF BASEBALL'S MOST COLORFUL AND
EXCITING STARS. EXCELLED IN ALL PHASES OF
THE GAME. THIRD IN HOMERS (660), RUNS (2,062)
AND TOTAL BASES (6,066); SEVENTH IN HITS
(3,283) AND RBI'S (1,903). FIRST IN PUTOUTS
BY OUTFIELDER (7,095). FIRST TO TOP BOTH
300 HOMERS AND 300 STEALS. LED LEAGUE IN
BATTING ONCE, SLUGGING FIVE TIMES,
RUNS AND STEALS FOUR SEASONS. VOT
MVP IN 1954 AND 1965. PLAYED
ALL-STAR GAMES - A RECO

This plaque commemorating Willie Mays hangs in the National Baseball Hall of
Fame at Cooperstown, New York.

you want. I chose baseball, and I loved every minute of it."

Willie has said that his plaque at the Hall of Fame in Cooperstown, New York, had barely begun gathering dust when he was forced out of baseball. Willie had taken a public relations job for Bally's Casino. Major League Baseball was afraid that it would reflect badly on them if one of its Hall of Fame players was working for a gambling casino. So baseball officials told Willie he had to make a choice. Willie chose Bally's.

The casino had offered him a ten-year contract that would pay him $100,000 a year. He needed the money, so he took the job. The money gave Willie the chance to sort out his finances. He used some of it to start a charity devoted to kids called the Say Hey Foundation. His foundation provides college scholarships to students who can't afford to pay for school.

In 1985, Peter Ueberroth, the commissioner of baseball, realized that Willie's job was not compromising the integrity of baseball or interfering with it in any way. So Willie was welcomed back.

Willie checks the swings of some young golfers at a Boys and Girls Club in Atlantic City, New Jersey. His Say Hey Foundation provides college scholarships to students.

Willie returned to the Giants in 1986. A man named Al Rosen had become president of the ball club. He wanted to restore some of the team pride from the 1950s and 1960s, when Willie was the starting center fielder.

Willie loved putting the Giants' uniform on again. He worked as a bench coach. Willie helped the players by talking with them and coaching them during pre-game workouts. He offered advice to the club's manager during games. In three years, the Giants went from finishing in last place to becoming playoff contenders.

Willie thinks he had something to do with it. He felt that he was able to motivate the younger players to play harder.

The 1987 season was one of the most thrilling ever for Willie. He got more excited watching the team fight for the pennant than when he was on the team!

Baseball was Willie Mays's life. From the time he was a kid watching his father play, nothing else seemed as important to him. To this day, there is nothing Willie Mays would rather do than be involved with baseball.

WILLIE MAYS *TIMELINE*

	May 6, 1931	Willie is born in Westfield, Alabama.
	1946	Willie plays professional baseball for the Birmingham Black Barons of the Negro National League.
	1947	Jackie Robinson becomes the first African American to play major league baseball in half a century. He faces a lot of adversity while playing for the Brooklyn Dodgers. Some people yell racial slurs while he is at bat or fielding balls.
	1948	Leo Durocher is hired as head coach of the New York Giants.
	1951	Willie is brought up from the minor leagues to play for the Giants. Durocher becomes Willie's mentor and good friend.
	1953	Willie's mother dies while giving birth to her eleventh child.
	1958	The Giants move from New York to San Francisco. Willie plays his first game in Seals Stadium.
	1960	Willie plays his first game in the Giants new home, Candlestick Park.

⚾	**1961**	Willie hits four home runs at County Stadium as the San Francisco Giants club the Milwaukee Braves, 14–4. (Mays is one of only twelve players in major league history ever to hit four homers in one game.) The Giants host the All-Star game, and Willie scores the game's winning run.
⚾	**1962**	Willie hits a home run in the last game of the season. The Giants win the game 2–1 and end up tied with the Dodgers for first place in the National League East. As in 1951, the teams are forced to play a three-game series to decide which one of them will advance into the playoffs. The Giants win the series and go on to beat the Yankees four games to three in the World Series.
⚾	May **1964**	Willie is named Giants team captain. He is the first African American team captain in baseball history.
⚾	**1970**	Willie hits his 600th career home run.
⚾	July **1970**	Willie gets his 3,000th hit.
⚾	May 12, **1972**	Willie is traded from the Giants to the New York Mets.
⚾	Sept. 25, **1973**	Willie retires from major league baseball.

Glossary

at bat   Each chance a player gets to hit the ball from home plate. Good ballplayers can be at bat 600 or more times in a season.

barnstorming   When a baseball team makes stops in small stadiums to play games on its way back from training camp.

batting   A hitter's ability to make contact with the baseball.

batting average   An average determined by dividing the number of base hits by the number of times at bat. The result is carried to three decimal places. A player with 100 base hits in 300 times at bat has a batting average of .333.

bunt   To push or tap the baseball lightly without swinging the bat. A player holds the bat parallel to the ground in an attempt to bounce the ball a few feet in front of home plate.

curve ball A medium speed pitch that drops several inches as it approaches home plate.

double A hit that allows the batter to reach second base safely.

fastball The most common pitch, normally thrown between 85 and 95 miles per hour. Batters can be confused between fastballs and changeups, which are thrown with the same motion as fastballs but travel at a much slower speed.

home run A hit that allows the batter to reach home plate safely and score a run. Most home runs are hit out of the field of play, but a hitter can also run around the bases to home plate before being tagged with the baseball.

inning A segment of a baseball game. Baseball games are divided into nine innings. There are six outs in each inning: three outs for each team.

juiced ball   A tightly wound baseball that travels farther and faster than a normal baseball when it is hit.

lead off   The first player to bat in an inning.

line drive   A hard hit ball that has low arc as it travels through the air. To hit a line drive, a batter must make excellent contact with the ball. Unless the ball is hit directly at a fielder, a line drive usually ends up as a base hit.

out   What the umpire calls when a batter fails to reach a base safely.

rookie   A first-year baseball player.

run batted in   A run that scores as a result of the batter. The batter is credited with an RBI if a runner scores. If the batter hits a fly ball that is caught in the outfield, he or she can still earn an RBI if the runner on third base is able to run home after the catch is made.

sacrifice   An intentional hit for an out so runners can advance to second or third base. Sacrifices are used when there are less than two outs, to increase a team's chances of scoring.

single A hit that allows the batter to reach first base safely.

slump An extended period of time during which a hitter plays below his or her potential.

stolen base A base obtained by running from one base to the next after a pitch is thrown. To steal a base safely, runners must be very fast. They must reach the base before getting thrown out by the catcher.

strike When a batter swings the bat and misses the ball, or when a pitcher throws a ball within the edges of home plate, between the batter's knees and chest. Batters are given three strikes before they are called out.

triple When the batter hits the ball and runs to third base safely.

veteran An experienced baseball player who has played for several years.

For More Information

National Baseball Hall of Fame Library
25 Main Street
P.O. Box 590
Cooperstown, NY 13326
(888) HALL OF FAME (425–5633)
Web site:
http://www.baseballhalloffame.org

Society for American Baseball Research
812 Huron Road, Suite 719
Cleveland, OH 44115
(216) 575-0500
Web site: www.sabr.org
e-mail: info@sabr.org

Say Hey Foundation
(650) 327-6297

Web Sites

Due to the changing nature of Internet links, the Rosen Publishing Group, Inc., has developed an online list of Web sites related to the subject of this book. This site is updated regularly. Please use this link to access the list:

http://www.rosenlinks.com/bbhf/wima/

For Further Reading

Burkhardt, Mitch. *Willie Mays*. Los Angeles, CA: Mass Market Paperback/Holloway House Publishing Company, 1991.

Grabowski, John. *Willie Mays*. New York: Chelsea House Publishers, 1990.

Hano, Arnold. *Willie Mays*. New York: Grossett & Dunlap, 1966.

Honig, Donald. *Mays, Mantle, Snider: A Celebration*. New York: Macmillan Publishing Co., 1987.

Mandel, Peter, and Don Tate. *Say Hey!* New York: Hyperion Books for Children, 2000.

Mays, Willie, and Charles Einstein. *Willie Mays: My Life In and Out of Baseball.* New York: E. P. Dutton, 1972.

Sabin, Louis. *Willie Mays: Young Superstar* (Easy Biographies). Mahwah, NJ: Troll Communications, 1999.

Bibliography

Einstein, Charles. *Willie's Time*. New York: J.B Lippincott Co., 1979.

Gutman, Bill. *Modern Baseball Superstars*. New York: Dodd, Mead & Co., 1973.

Hano, Arnold. *A Day in the Bleachers*. New York: Da Capo Press, 1982.

Mays, Willie, and Maxine Berger. *Willie Mays: 'Play Ball.'* New York: Simon and Schuster, 1980.

Mays, Willie, and Howard Liss. *My Secrets of Playing Baseball*. New York: The Viking Press, 1967.

Mays, Willie, and Lou Sahadi. *Say Hey.*
New York: Pocket Books, 1988.

Rossi, John P., *A Whole New Game: Off the
Field Changes in Baseball, 1946–1960.*
Jefferson, NC: McFarland & Co., 1999.

Rust, Art, Jr., *Get That Nigger Off the
Field!: A Sparkling, Informal History of
the Black Man in Baseball.* New York:
Delacorte Press, 1976.

Index

W

About the Author

Shaun McCormack, who lives in New Jersey, graduated from Montclair State University in Montclair. A baseball lover since his grandfather took him to his first game at age five, Shaun has also written *Cool Papa Bell* for the Rosen Publishing Group, Inc.

Photo Credits

Cover © AP/Wide World Photos; pp. 2, 3 © Eyewire Royalty Free; pp. 4, 8, 24, 33, 38–39, 46–47, 52, 55, 58, 62, 81, 84, 92 © AP/Wide World Photos; p. 7 © Topps Baseball Inc.; pp. 12, 15, 66, 68, 70, 76–77, 83, 87, 89 © Bettmann/Corbis; p. 18 © Lucien Aigher/Corbis; p. 43 © J.R. Eyerman/TimePix; p. 90 © Ray Stubblebine/AP/Wide World Photos; p. 94 © Chris Polk/AP/Wide World Photos; pp. 5, 9, 25, 41, 50, 73, 86, 96–97, 98, 102, 104, 106, 108 © Corbis Royalty Free.

Editor

Jill Jarnow

Series Design and Layout

Geri Giordano